SCUBA ADVENTURE

Written by: Chris Vozzo

Illustrated by Nina Mkhoiani

1st edition 2024

For everyone in the trades that build the
infrastructure for our communities to thrive.

POSEIDON
PLUMBING

In the coastal town where Poseidon,
the friendly plumber, was vacationing, there was a buzz
of excitement in the air. Poseidon was about to embark on
an adventure beneath the sparkling waves. He equipped
his blue and yellow scuba suit and underwater tool belt.
His special scuba suit and tool belt made him confident.

POSEIDON
PLUMBING
POSEIDON
PLUMBING

With a wave to his friends on the shore, he descended into the cool embrace of the ocean. Bubbles escaped from his regulator, creating a symphony of underwater sounds as Poseidon explored the wonders below.

The sea greeted Poseidon with open arms, revealing a mesmerizing world of colorful coral reefs and playful sea creatures. Schools of fish swirled around him, and curious sea turtles glided gracefully through the water.

The sea creatures made him feel welcome in their watery world. An eel even greeted him as he drifted by. Poseidon, with his scuba mask snugly in place, marveled at the beauty of the underwater realm.

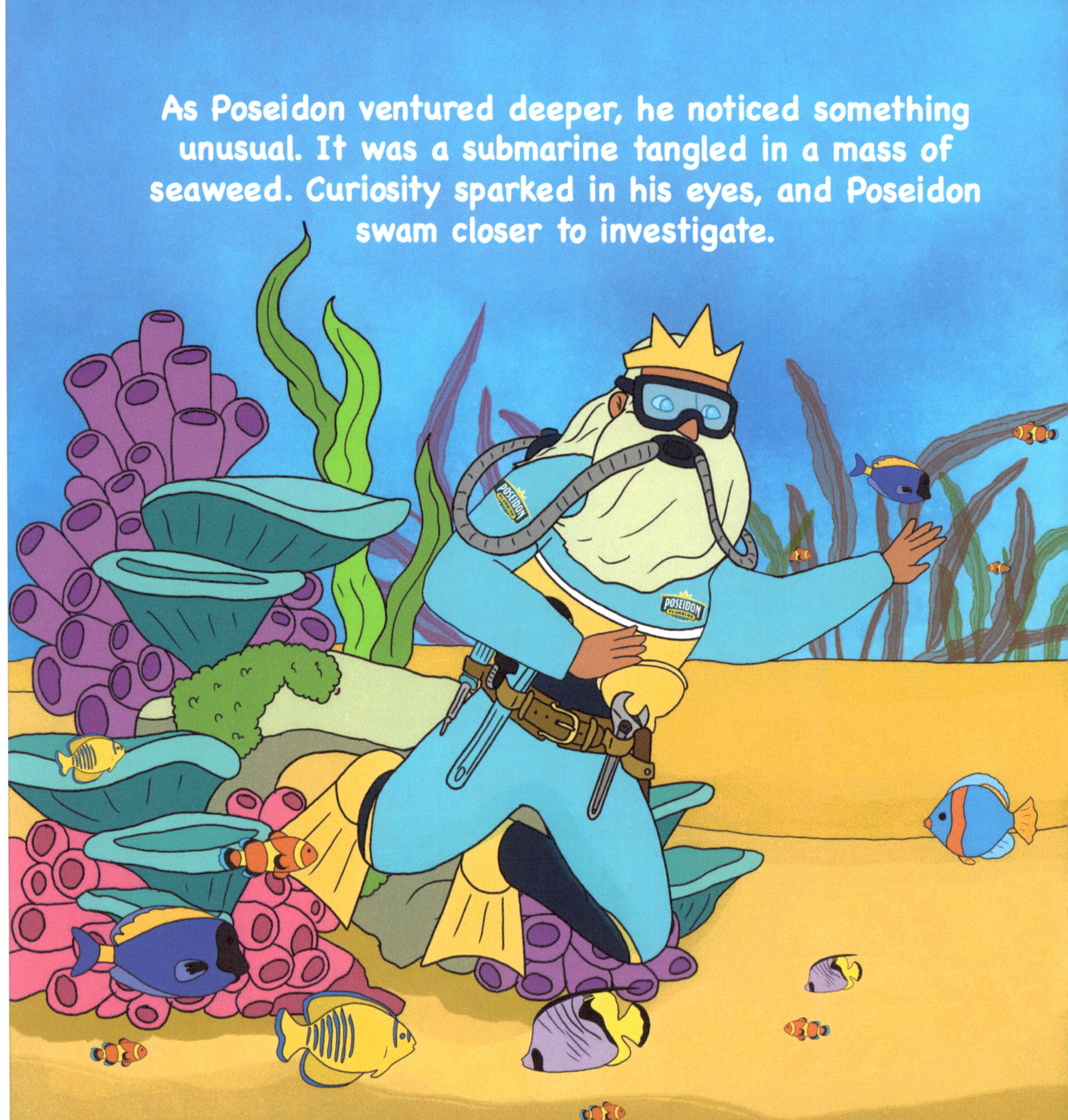

As Poseidon ventured deeper, he noticed something unusual. It was a submarine tangled in a mass of seaweed. Curiosity sparked in his eyes, and Poseidon swam closer to investigate.

To his surprise, he discovered that the submarine
was leaking water. Its pumps were working as hard as
they could, but the water was coming in too fast.
A plumbing problem in the heart of the ocean!

Determined to lend a helping hand,
Poseidon reached into his tool belt and pulled out his
trusty pipe wrench. With a few expert twists and turns,
he tightened the loose bolts, sealing the leak.

POSEIDON
PLUMBING

The water inside of the submarine gradually cleared,
and Poseidon, the plumber turned underwater hero,
successfully resolved the plumbing issue. Poseidon bid
farewell to the submarine crew and continued his journey.

The news of Poseidon's feat quickly spread through the ocean depths, reaching the ears of a friendly octopus named Oliver. Eager for Poseidon's help, Oliver approached with frantic excitement.

He asked him to help in a hidden underwater cave.
Poseidon agreed to help if Oliver would be his
underwater helper. Intrigued, Poseidon followed
his new friend.

Inside the cave, Poseidon discovered a bustling underwater village. The inhabitants, a community of sea creatures, were facing their own plumbing problem.

It was a clogged drainpipe. Poseidon, ever ready for a challenge, assessed the situation. With his knowledge and trusty plunger, he dove into action, clearing the pipe and restoring the flow of water to the city.

The grateful sea creatures, from chatty seahorses to wise old lobsters, cheered for Poseidon's plumbing prowess.

The news of his underwater plumbing adventures spread far and wide, reaching even the depths of the ocean where the elusive mermaids lived. Oliver the Octopus was so amazed that he continued to learn about the plumbing trade and became Poseidon's new apprentice.

As Poseidon said goodbye to his new friends,
he noticed a magical glow in the distance. It led him to
a garden of bioluminescent coral, where vibrant colors
illuminated the ocean floor.

Poseidon, with a sense of calm, realized that his scuba adventure had not only been about discovering the enchanting beauty hidden beneath the waves but also that helping those in need made him happy.

With a content heart, Poseidon resurfaced and swam back to the shore. His friends welcomed him with cheers, unaware of the underwater exploits that had taken place.

Poseidon shared tales of his scuba adventure, helping the
magical underwater city become lore.

POSEIDON
PLUMBING

And so, Poseidon continued to be a hero both on land and beneath the sea. His scuba adventure became a legendary tale, inspiring children and sea creatures to appreciate the importance of helping each other in times of need and the magic that could be found in the most unexpected places.

INTERACTIVE QUESTIONS

1.   Exploring the Ocean Depths: "If you could join Poseidon on his underwater adventure, which sea creature would you be most excited to see and why? Would you like to swim with playful dolphins, observe colorful fish, or find a hidden octopus like Oliver?"

2.   Poseidon's Tools and Skills: "Poseidon used his plumbing tools to fix problems under the sea. If you had a special tool belt like Poseidon, what tools would you put in it for your underwater adventures, and how would you use them to help sea creatures?"

3.   Discovering Underwater Cities: "Poseidon found a bustling underwater village with sea creatures living together. What do you think an underwater village looks like? What kinds of buildings or homes would sea creatures have?"

4.   Helping Under the Sea: "Poseidon helped fix a leak in a submarine and unclogged a pipe in the underwater village. Can you think of another problem that might happen underwater that Poseidon could help solve with his plumbing skills?"

5.   The Magic of the Ocean: "At the end of his adventure, Poseidon discovered a garden of bioluminescent coral. What do you think makes the ocean magical? Can you imagine and describe a magical sea creature or plant that Poseidon might find on his next adventure?"